ASTHMA

MONA KERBY

ASTHMA

Franklin Watts
New York / London / Toronto / Sydney / 1989
A Venture Book

Photographs courtesy of:
The Bettmann Archive: pp. 12, 39 (both);
UPI/Bettmann Newsphotos: pp. 15, 16, 55;
80 (Yoav Levy); Rita Rooney: p. 23 (top);
Photo Researchers: pp. 23 (bottom, Robert
Goldstein), 30 (top left), 30 (bottom left,
Science Photo Library), 30 (top right,
Asa Thoresen), 30 (bottom right) and 32
(Dr. Jeremy Burgess/SPL), 34 (top, SPL),
34 (bottom), 44 (John Durham/SPL), 47
(Mary Evans Picture Library), 62 (Susan
Leavines); The American Lung Association
of Colorado's Champ Camp Program: p. 65;
HealthScan Products: p. 69; MedicAlert: p. 77.

Library of Congress Cataloging-in-Publication Data

Kerby, Mona.
Asthma.

(A Venture book)
Bibliography: p.
Includes index.
Summary: Discusses the different kinds of asthma,
their causes, and remedies for asthma attacks.
1. Asthma—Juvenile literature. [1. Asthma] I. Title.
RC591.K46 1989   616.2'38   89-8905
ISBN 0-531-10697-7

CONTENTS

*I am grateful for the help
of the following people:*

*Librarian Frances Brown
and the staff of the
Meadowbrook branch
of the Fort Worth Public
Library for their pleasant
and efficient assistance;*

*Maury Solomon for
her editorial expertise;*

*and most especially
my students Wendell,
Michael, Brandon, and
Brad for their willingness
to share their own
experiences in coping
with asthma.*

INTRODUCTION

As one of the most common childhood diseases, asthma affects between 5 and 10 percent of the children in the United States. Because of asthma, American students miss 125 million school days yearly. In fact, asthma is the leading cause of school absenteeism—61.3 percent of the days missed are the direct result of it.

Asthma can strike suddenly and severely and then disappear for weeks at a time. The most ordinary of events can trigger an attack that can, in rare cases, be fatal if untreated. With good reason, many people with asthma are terrified of wind, trees, perfume, or even their own laughter.

This does not have to be so. Although asthma is not curable, it is one of the most treatable conditions in the world. And attacks can usually be prevented. The purpose of this book is to provide information that will promote prevention and proper treatment.

Famous People with Asthma

Sometimes, people wish their lives were different. If you have asthma, you might have said to yourself many times, "If only I didn't have asthma, my life would be so wonderful." And perhaps it would be better.

But some of the world's greatest figures have had serious medical problems. In fact, they may have become great because they were able to turn their problems into strengths—through determination. They refused to quit. As a result, they succeeded in achieving their dreams and left their mark on the world.

There are many famous people who have suffered from asthma. Writers, actors, dancers, and even a president of the United States have had the disease. Surprisingly, many famous athletes have suffered from asthma, also.

Theodore Roosevelt

Theodore Roosevelt (1858–1919) was president of the United States from 1901 to 1909. He assumed office after President William McKinley was assassinated in September 1901, and was elected to a full term in 1904.

Roosevelt was an extremely popular president. He was called "Teddy" by millions of Americans. This strong, energetic man enjoyed hunting, horseback riding, swimming, hiking, and boxing. Toymakers named the teddy bear after him.

As a child growing up in New York, Roosevelt was frequently ill. He suffered from severe asthma. At times, he was picked on by other boys because he was too puny to fight back. When he was twelve, his father told him that a good mind required a strong body. He built his son a gymnasium in the basement of their home, and Roosevelt exercised regularly, eventually conquering his asthma and becoming exceptionally strong.

After Roosevelt graduated from Harvard in 1880, he served as a legislator in New York State. But he quit in 1884 when both his wife and mother died on the same day. He traveled west to the Dakota territory and worked as a cowboy. He also wrote books.

In 1896, he returned to New York, remarried, and resumed his career in public service. In 1898, he led the Rough Riders during the Spanish-American War and became a national hero.

During Roosevelt's years as president, he negotiated the building of the Panama Canal. He also declared that the U. S. government in its foreign policy should "talk softly but carry a big stick," or be prepared to use force whenever necessary but not make idle threats.

In later years, after he retired, Roosevelt explored some of the world's remaining wildernesses. In 1918, while in the Brazilian jungle, he became ill with jungle fever, and he died at home in New York in 1919.

Marcel Proust

Marcel Proust (1871–1922) is considered one of the greatest French novelists of the twentieth century. His masterpiece was a seven-part novel entitled *Remembrance of Things Past*.

Proust helped change the form of the French novel. His techniques included long sentences and a poetic style. Proust's characters seemed extraordinarily real. Through them, he painted vivid pictures of love and jealousy.

Proust grew up in Paris. He developed asthma when he was nine, and he suffered with it the rest of his life. His mother tenderly cared for him. According to Proust, no woman could ever equal his mother.

As an adult, Proust did not take care of himself. He didn't sleep much, and he ate little. He tried to treat his asthma using strange remedies, such as drinking cold beer. After catching cold, Proust died from his disease in the summer of 1922.

Robert Joffrey

Robert Joffrey (1930–1988) was an American ballet dancer, teacher, and choreographer (composer of dances). The company he founded, the Joffrey Ballet, is considered one of the top three ballet companies in America.

Joffrey, named by his parents Abdullah Jaffa Anver Bey Khan, was born in Seattle. His father was from Afghanistan, and his mother was from Italy. He

Theodore Roosevelt overcame asthma to lead the Rough Riders during the Spanish-American War and, eventually, become president of the United States.

began dancing as a young boy after a doctor suggested that it might improve his asthma.

In 1956, the Joffrey Ballet started with a borrowed station wagon and six dancers. While they toured America, Joffrey worked in New York to pay for the tour. Over the years, Joffrey's company traveled to small towns and cities all over the country. Because of Joffrey, thousands of Americans were able to enjoy ballet for the first time. The company has also toured the Middle East, the Far East, and the Soviet Union and has performed at the White House.

The Joffrey Ballet company performs a wide variety of works, from traditional to modern dance. In his 1967 *Astarte,* a couple danced to rock-and-roll music in front of a billowing white silk curtain while a movie of the couple dancing was projected on the curtain.

Joffrey died of a liver ailment in 1988, caused by medication he was taking for his severe asthma.

Robert Donat

Robert Donat (1905–1958) was a famous English actor. In 1939, he won an Academy Award for his role as the English teacher in the movie, *Goodbye, Mr. Chips.*

Donat was tall and had a deep voice. He had leading roles in *The Inn of the Sixth Happiness, The Thirty-nine Steps, The Magic Box, The Winslow Boy, The Young Mr. Pitts, The Ghost Goes West, Knight Without Armor,* and *Citadel.*

Donat suffered with severe asthma. In spite of poor health throughout his acting career, he continued to work.

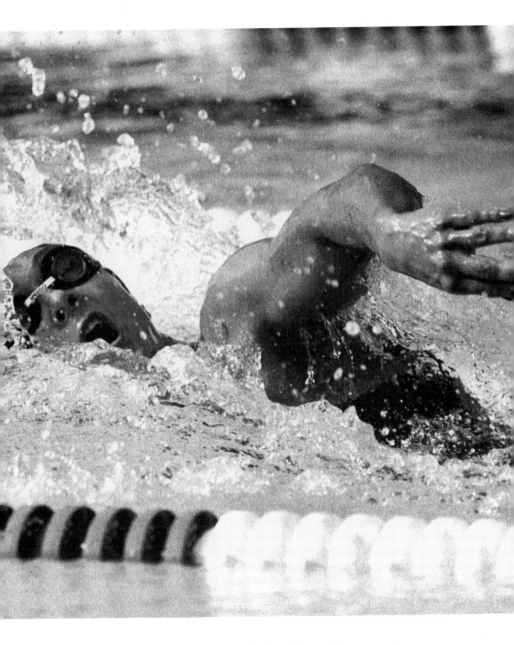

*Olympic gold-medalist Nancy Hogshead
swims—and wins—despite asthma.*

Olympic Athletes

At the 1984 Summer Olympic Games, the American team was composed of 597 athletes. Of that number 11 percent, or 67 members, of the team suffered from asthma. Forty-one of them won medals.

The athletes with asthma participated in a wide variety of sports. They included cyclists Alexi Grewal, Bill Nitts, and Steve Hegg; sprinter Jeanette Bolden; Greco-Roman wrestler Dave Schultz; volleyball player Paula Weishoff; and basketball player Sam Perkins. Swimmer Nancy Hogshead carried home three gold medals and one silver medal.

There were eight athletes with asthma in the 1984 Winter Olympic team. Team member Bill Koch, who also won medals in 1980, is considered one of the best cross-country skiers in the world. At the 1988 Summer Olympics, Jackie Joyner-Kersee, who also has asthma, won the gold medal in the women's heptathalon event.

The Olympic athletes take their medication regularly and have learned to manage their asthma, although they still have occasional attacks that cost them points in competition.

*Athlete Jackie Joyner-Kersee,
asthma sufferer, won the
gold medal in the women's
heptathalon at the 1988
Summer Olympics.*

CHAPTER

1

WHAT IS ASTHMA?

Defining Asthma

Asthma, also known as bronchial asthma and asth-matic bronchitis, is a medical condition that involves a difficulty in breathing. It occurs when the airways of the lungs constrict (tighten). Victims, gasping for air, feel as if they are suffocating. Often unpredict-able, attacks, also called *flareups* or *episodes*, may last for a few minutes, a few hours, or days. Symp-toms range from mild to severe.

The act of breathing provides our bodies with a continuous supply of oxygen. This oxygen is used to process the food we eat to obtain energy for living, growing, and other tasks. About one-fifth of the air that enters our bodies is oxygen, which is breathed into the lungs and absorbed into the bloodstream. The blood carries the oxygen from the lungs to the various cells of the body, which use it up and produce, as a waste product, the gas carbon dioxide, which is sent back to the lungs and exhaled.

As you breathe in, or inhale, air flows through your nose or mouth down the throat *(pharynx)*. It passes through the voicebox *(larynx)* and then enters the windpipe *(trachea)*. The air then reaches the lungs' two *bronchial tubes,* or *bronchi,* also known as the large airways. It then moves into smaller structures, or branches, of the bronchial tubes known as the *bronchioles,* or small airways. Finally, the air reaches the 300 million or so air sacs, called *alveoli,* where an exchange of oxygen and carbon dioxide takes place. The oxygen is carried by tiny capillaries, or thin blood vessels, to the bodies' cells and tissues; and the carbon dioxide leaves your body when you breathe out, or exhale.

The diaphragm, located between the chest cavity and the stomach area, is the main muscle used for breathing. It normally contracts (pulls in) when you breathe in, creating a kind of vacuum that draws air into the lungs. When the diaphragm relaxes, this vacuum disappears, and air leaves the lungs.

Hairs in the nose trap large particles of dust, preventing them from reaching the lungs. Mucus, a sticky fluid produced by glands in the nose, traps finer particles. Hairlike structures, called *cilia,* move the dirty mucus out of the nose. Particles coated with mucus that reach the bronchioles are captured by tiny cilia there and are moved toward the pharynx, where they are either swallowed or coughed up.

People with asthma have "twitchy," or spastic, airways. Certain triggers, such as allergies, exercise,

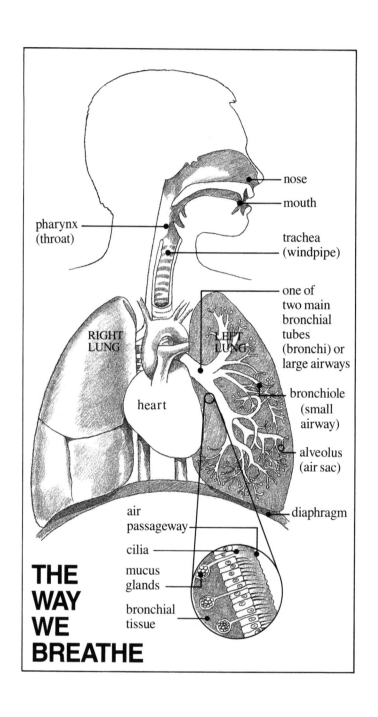

nose

mouth

pharynx
(throat)

trachea
(windpipe)

one of
two main
bronchial
tubes
(bronchi) or
large airways

RIGHT
LUNG

LEFT
LUNG

bronchiole
(small
airway)

heart

alveolus
(air sac)

diaphragm

air
passageway

cilia

mucus
glands

bronchial
tissue

**THE
WAY
WE
BREATHE**

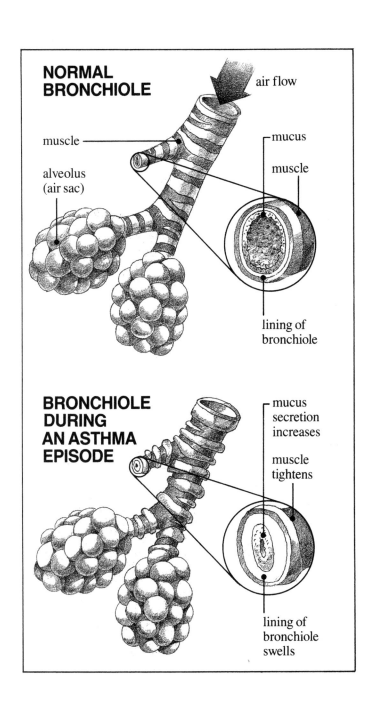

NORMAL BRONCHIOLE

air flow

muscle

alveolus (air sac)

mucus

muscle

lining of bronchiole

BRONCHIOLE DURING AN ASTHMA EPISODE

mucus secretion increases

muscle tightens

lining of bronchiole swells

viral infections, airborne irritants, and strong emotions provoke an asthmatic response, which is really an overreaction to the environment. The tendency to develop asthma seems to be inherited. Asthma cannot be "caught," it is not a contagious disease.

A bronchial spasm—the twitching—can start in all of the airways or in one section of the lungs. The trigger sets off a chain reaction of events. Almost immediately, one of the spasmodic airways begins to constrict (tighten). This constriction causes the airways to swell, which in turn makes them smaller. Breathing becomes difficult. Air forced through the narrow passages produces a high-pitched, rattling whistle, called wheezing. At the same time, the swollen airways produce mucus. This mucus may become so sticky that plugs of it form and completely block the air passages. The person reacts by coughing. Although the coughing tends to be dry, it may still bring up lots of mucus.

The combination of constriction, swelling, and mucus creates a serious situation. In an attempt to get more air, the person with asthma breathes rapidly, taking shallow, labored breaths. However, he or she is unable to breathe in oxygen through the blocked passages and exhale the stale air. The lungs enlarge. Nostrils flare. When inhaling, the ribs pull in instead of expanding. The neck muscles bulge and tighten. Blood pressure swings up and down. The heart races.

In severe cases, the person with asthma flushes, perspires, shows signs of cyanosis (bluish skin), appears confused, and has broken speech. As the attack progresses, the person is overwhelmed by anxiety and

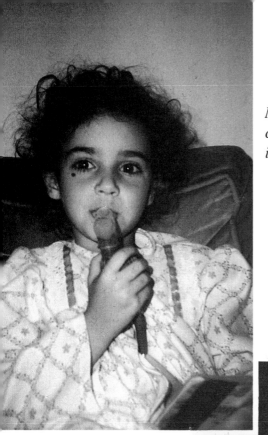

Most children learn to control their asthma and, in time, outgrow it.

Severe attacks require medical treatment.

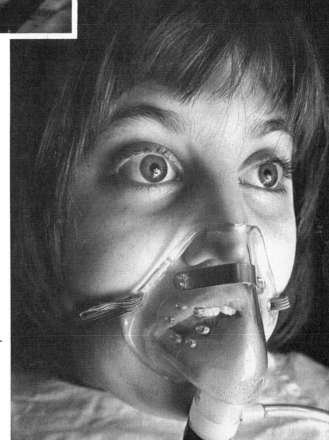

fatigue. Although rare, death can result if the attack is not halted. In the United States, there are about a hundred deaths annually due to asthma in children one to fifteen years old. About two-thirds of the children with asthma significantly improve or outgrow the disease by their teens, possibly because of growth in the diameter of the windpipe.

Asthma has two surprising additional features. First, between attacks, people with asthma frequently show no signs of the disease. Second, even violent attacks do not seem to cause serious damage. Long-term effects include a slight increase in the size of the mucus-producing glands and a slight thickening of the muscle cells surrounding the airways.

Kinds of Asthma

The term *extrinsic asthma* is used to describe attacks caused by a known trigger. It is usually an allergic reaction to substances in the environment. Extrinsic asthma can be diagnosed by skin tests and is associated with hay fever and the skin condition eczema. This kind of asthma usually disappears with childhood.

The term *intrinsic asthma* describes asthma in which the external cause is unknown. Intrinsic asthma cannot be diagnosed by skin tests. The age of onset (when it starts) is usually after the age of twenty-five, although it is also occasionally found in children.

Mixed asthma describes asthma that may have both intrinsic and extrinsic elements.

Features of Asthma

From 2 to 20 percent of the world's population may experience asthma in their lifetime. Although asthma is found all over the world, it is a major health problem only in industrialized countries. There are differences among populations. At least 9 million Americans have asthma, many of them black Americans who live in poor urban neighborhoods. Asthma is rare among West Africans, American Indians, and Eskimos. Nearly 30 percent of the people on the island of Trinidad suffer from asthma.

Asthma can strike at any age. However, most attacks begin before the age of fifteen or after the age of forty-five. Approximately half of childhood asthma cases occur by the age of three.

Asthma is common in children because their airways are small and because they have not yet developed a wide variety of immunities to infection. Even though most children will outgrow asthma, it can resurface later in life.

If the first attack occurs before the age of five or after the age of twenty, it is more than likely to be intrinsic asthma, which is rarely outgrown. If the onset occurs between ages five and twenty, it is usually extrinsic asthma.

In English-speaking countries, 30 percent of asthma sufferers report that their asthma began before the age of ten. In Finland, 42 percent of asthma sufferers reported that their first symptoms occurred after the age of forty-five.

Asthma is three times more common in boys than in girls. Boys have more severe attacks than girls. After puberty (sexual maturity), the attacks become more equal between the sexes. As adults, more women than men develop asthma.

Myths About Asthma

In the twentieth century, many physicians and psychiatrists mistakenly promoted certain ideas concerning asthma. Unfortunately, some people still accept these myths as fact. The following statements are completely false:

- Emotional disorders cause asthma.
- Asthma is a psychosomatic ("all in the mind") disease.
- People with asthma have highly nervous or neurotic personalities.
- People with asthma have an abnormal relationship with their mothers.

Even though emotions can trigger asthma, a person must first have a malfunction in their lungs before the attack can occur.

Diseases that Resemble Asthma

Several illnesses are similar in appearance to asthma. These include croup, pneumonia, bronchitis, bronchiolitis, emphysema, foreign objects in the lung, and cystic fibrosis. Coughing, wheezing, and difficulty in breathing are common characteristics of these conditions.

If you think you might have asthma, do *not* attempt to diagnose or treat yourself. Seek medical attention. With a doctor's care and prescribed medications, you can usually expect to keep your asthma under control. Most people with asthma can expect to lead full and active lives.

CHAPTER

2

MORE ABOUT
ASTHMA TRIGGERS

For most asthma patients, the specific causes of their asthmatic attacks are unknown. As a result, it is difficult to predict what will trigger an attack. However, for other patients, the triggers are known. These include allergies, exercise, viral infections, and stress. Knowledge about these triggers and their relationship to asthma can prevent or lessen the severity of the attacks for some patients.

Allergies

An *allergen* is any substance that produces an allergic reaction, which is an overreaction by the body's immune system to a foreign substance. To produce this reaction, allergens may be either inhaled or ingested (eaten). Allergens trigger asthma attacks because the particles that make them up are usually too small to be filtered out by the nose or the pharynx, and are present in high amounts for a relatively long time. Unfortunately, after a person becomes "sensitive" to an allergen, even small amounts of it will provoke an attack.

When confronted with the allergen, the white blood cells of a person with asthma immediately begin to manufacture antibodies in order to protect the body against the perceived invaders. The resulting allergic symptoms range from stuffy nose, watery eyes, and scratchy throat to swellings on the body, migraine headaches, hives, coughing, itchy skin, and breathing difficulty. Anaphylaxis, a severe allergic reaction, can result in death. Allergies do not invariably trigger asthmatic attacks. Still, it makes sense to avoid known allergens whenever possible.

Pollen
Pollen is a fine yellowish powder produced by flowering plants, grasses, weeds, and trees. Plants pollinated by the wind cause far more allergy problems than plants pollinated by insects.

Grasses pollinate from spring through summer. Allergy-prone individuals are usually sensitive to all grasses, with the exception of Bermuda grass. Weeds pollinate from late spring through fall. Ragweed provokes more allergic reactions than any other weed. Trees pollinate from late winter through spring. Most people are not allergic to all trees, but specific kinds will provoke allergy symptoms.

Weather conditions during pollination determine

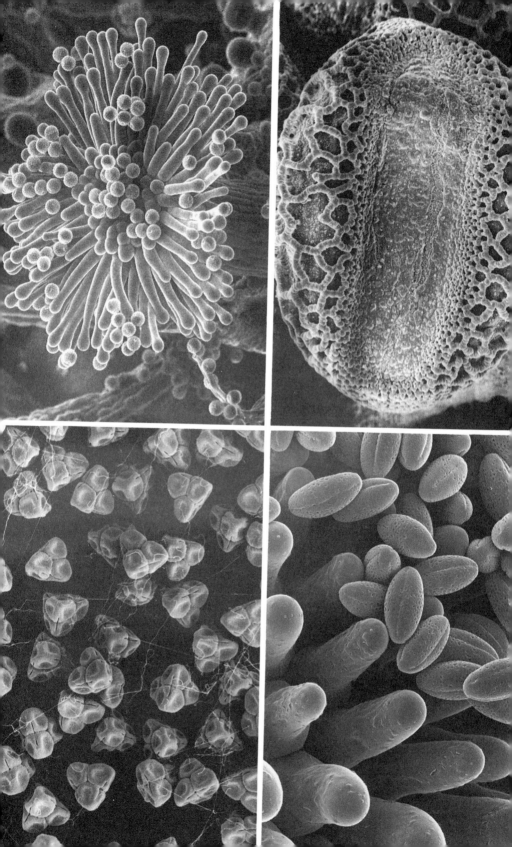

the length and severity of allergic reactions. The worst allergic reactions occur when there is rain before the pollination season and strong winds during it. Ideal weather conditions for allergy sufferers occur when there is wind and dryness before the season and when there is rain during the season.

Fungus

A fungus is any one of a group of plants that has no leaves or flowers and is usually not green in color. Examples are molds, mushrooms, dry rot, mildew, and plant rust. These hardy parasites grow everywhere, on both living and nonliving materials.

Fungi reproduce rapidly by means of tiny particles called *spores*. Spores travel through the air. In every breath you take, there may be millions of mold spores. Allergic reactions can occur whenever the spores of a fungi are inhaled or ingested.

Outdoors, fungi can grow on plants and in soil, hay, mulches, commercial peat moss, compost piles, leaf litter, and commercial crops. They thrive in humid climates. After a lawn is mowed, millions of fungi spores can be found in the air.

Pollen grains cause
many allergy symptoms.
Clockwise from upper
left, magnified, are:
ragweed, Easter lily,
turnip flower, and
rhododendron.

Spores circulate in the air and alight where they can grow—here (greatly magnified) the globelike shape is a mold growing on bread.

Fungi live year-round indoors. Mold flourishes in water vaporizers, humidifiers, air conditioners, hot-air systems, refrigerator drip trays, window moldings, shower curtains, and cold, moist basements. Fungi can grow on food that's been left out as well as on refrigerated food stored for as little as three days.

Animals
Allergic reactions to animals are common. Cats, dogs, and horses—in that order—provoke the most frequent

reactions. People are not usually allergic to animal hair. Rather, they are allergic to the animal *dander,* the dead skin that flakes off the animal. They are also allergic to the animal's saliva. Because cats lick themselves so often, they cause more allergic reactions than other animals do. And because animal dander becomes part of household dust, sensitive people will still suffer from allergic reactions even if the animal is removed for a while. In addition to pets, feather pillows aggravate allergies. Finally, filthy living conditions trigger allergies. Allergens are found in rat and mice urine and also in cockroach feces.

Mites

Mites are tiny arachnids (spiders) that usually live on plants or on other animals. Mites like to feed on human skin particles that have been shed. Thus, they also live and multiply in mattresses, pillows, and carpets. They are abundant in damp houses. Research indicates that the feces of mites may be one of the most highly toxic allergens.

Dust

Household dust is a combination of animal dander, mites, molds, fungi, food particles, pollen, bacteria, human skin cells, dirt, insect parts, and feces. All of these can be allergens.

Odors

Odors can apparently trigger asthmatic attacks. In one study, 95 percent of volunteers with asthma experi-

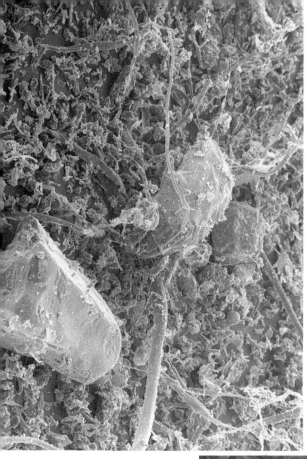

This magnified sample of household dust shows a dust mite sprawling at the center, surrounded by a particle of grit and skin scales, fibers, cat fur, and soil particles.

Sand and grit particles, skin scales, fibers, cat fur, and flea droppings appear in this magnified dust sample. The smooth oval in the center is a cat-flea egg.

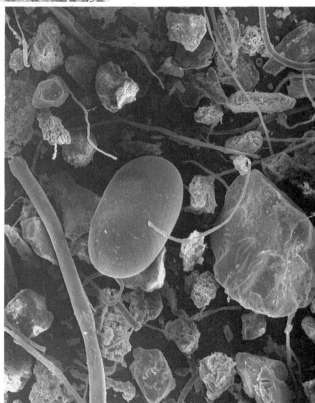

enced a reaction to odors. The most offensive odors were insecticides. Next were household cleaners, particularly those with ammonia. Perfumes and fresh paints affected 75 percent of the volunteers; car exhaust and gas fumes affected 50 percent of the volunteers; and cooking smells affected 33 percent of the volunteers.

Other allergens that can trigger asthma attacks include cigarette and cigar smoke, newsprint, powdered enzymes, wood dust, and chemicals used in the plastics industry.

Food

Food allergies play a much smaller role in triggering asthma attacks than do environmental allergies. It is estimated that only 10 percent of children with asthma and 5 percent of adults with asthma have attacks as a result of their food allergies. Allergies to some foods such as milk, wheat, corn, and eggs are often outgrown, whereas allergies to fish (particularly shellfish) and nuts tend to endure. Products that include aspirin, acetaminophen, monosodium glutamate, sulfiting agents, and tartrazine (Yellow Food Dye #5) can produce allergic reactions.

Particular food and environmental allergies can be identified through the use of blood tests, scratch tests, and food elimination diets. For a scratch test, the substance believed to be the allergen is placed on a small, scratched section of the patient's skin. During a food elimination diet, specific foods are avoided in order to determine whether or not they are the offending allergens.

One method of controlling allergens is by getting allergy shots, but the best method is to avoid the known allergens altogether. Cleanliness and diet are important. Later chapters give additional suggestions for controlling allergies and other factors that trigger asthma.

Exercise

Exercise can trigger asthma under two conditions: when the exercise is strenuous and when the air is cool. People breathe through their mouths after vigorous exercise. As a result, the air has not been warmed and humidified by the nose. This cool, dry air may trigger the asthma symptoms. (See Chapter 4 for more on exercise.)

Infections

Asthma patients are susceptible to respiratory infections. Viral infections such as the common cold frequently lead to asthma symptoms. In fact, the first appearance of asthma often occurs with a viral infection.

Stress

As stated earlier, if you have asthma, it does not mean you have psychological problems. The tendency to develop asthma is often inherited. However, if you do have asthma, stress can affect the frequency and severity of attacks.

CHAPTER

3

MEDICATIONS

People have suffered from asthma for thousands of years. Written records from ancient civilizations name the disease, identify its symptoms, and suggest remedies. A few of these remedies are still in use today.

Early Treatments

The word *asthma* comes from the ancient Greeks. In their language, asthma was a verb that meant "to pant" or "to breathe hard." As early as 25 B.C., Celsus described asthmatic wheeze: "On account of the narrow passages by which the air escapes, it comes out as a whistle."

Four or five thousand years ago, the Chinese were using ephedrine to treat asthma. This herbal remedy relieved coughs and colds. Soon after the first century, ephedrine was forgotten. It was not used again until the twentieth century, when it was rediscovered.

One folk remedy for asthma that has been passed down among families for generations is garlic. When garlic is crushed, a pungent aroma is released. This aroma is said to stimulate mucus production. Horseradish, radishes, onions, hot peppers, and mustard produce similar results.

Another old folk remedy is hot chicken soup. It was first prescribed in the twelfth century by Maimonides. In his *Treatise on Asthma,* he apologizes for not having a cure but suggests that "the soup of fat hens is [an] effective remedy."

By the seventeenth century, Europeans were using plants containing atropine. The leaves of plants such as the stinkweed or the thorn apple were smoked until the cough was reduced.

Coffee and tea have also been used to relieve asthmatic symptoms. Caffeine is a *bronchodilator,* meaning that it opens up the passages of the lungs. Even today, a cup of tea or strong coffee is sometimes recommended to relieve the symptoms of asthma.

Although garlic, hot chicken soup, and coffee may not have great medicinal value, they are relatively harmless and can provide slight relief. Other treatments, however, are no longer recommended.

At least one physician prescribed alcohol to treat asthma. In 1863, Dr. Henry Hyde published the results of his work with three asthma patients. He stated that the patients' symptoms were relieved by drinking large amounts of whiskey, gin, and brandy. To his credit, Hyde warned against the overuse of alcohol. The dangerous possible side effects of alcohol and alcoholism make this an unsatisfactory treatment.

*Old patent medicines promised relief
from asthma and many other ailments.*

Gold is another outdated medical treatment. For centuries, many people thought that gold had magical healing powers. In the late 1800s, there were gold treatments for tuberculosis, arthritis, and asthma. By the 1930s, gold treatments were stopped because of the serious side effects of bone-marrow poisoning and blood loss through the urine.

One drug that is rarely used today is ephedrine. After the Japanese rediscovered it, ephedrine became one of the most important drugs in treating asthma. Taken orally, it served as a weak-acting bronchodilator. But ephedrine's side effects were often harder to tolerate than the actual asthmatic symptoms.

Isoproteronal was developed in the 1940s and became the most commonly used inhalation product. It brought relief within minutes, although its effectiveness wore off within hours. Because of its serious side effects, isoproteronal is rarely prescribed today.

Modern Medications

Modern medications for asthma attempt to do two things: (1) relieve symptoms and (2) prevent new attacks. In this section, medications that are currently used in the United States to treat asthma will be described. After reading this section, you will have a general overview of asthma medications. For specific treatments for yourself, consult your physician. DO NOT USE THIS INFORMATION TO SELF-MEDICATE.

Theophylline

In the United States today, theophylline is the most frequently used drug in asthma-medication programs.

Chemically similar to caffeine, theophylline relaxes the bronchial smooth muscle. As a result, the airways are opened and breathing becomes easier. Theophylline stimulates the clearance of mucus from the airways. It can even prevent wheezing from developing.

Theophylline is taken orally, usually in capsules or tablets. It is also available as "sprinkles" for young children who have difficulty swallowing pills. The capsule is opened and the medication is sprinkled over pudding or applesauce.

Theophylline is used for a wide range of asthma symptoms. Patients with severe asthma take a long-acting theophylline on a daily basis. Patients who have asthma attacks infrequently and have no symptoms between attacks take a short-acting theophylline at the time of the attack. One or two hours elapse before all the symptoms are relieved. Possible side effects include increased heart rate, nausea, and frequent urination.

Some of the brand names for long-acting theophylline include: Constant T, Slo-Bid Gyrocaps, Sustaire, Theo-dur, and Theo 24. Some brandnames for short-acting theophylline include: Bronkodyl, Elixicon, Slo-Phyllin, Elixophyllin, and Theophyl.

Epinephrine
In the 1860s, a London physician noted that intense excitement or stress could ease asthma attacks. Today we know that in periods of stress, the adrenal glands release the hormone epinephrine, also known as adrenaline. This hormone produces several changes in the body and prepares the body for "fight or flight." Epinephrine provides quick relief for acute asthma at-

tacks by relaxing the muscles in the large airways leading to the lungs.

Since the 1920s, epinephrine has been chemically synthesized. This medication is used only in emergency treatment. It is injected under the skin. If relief does not occur within twenty minutes, another injection may be given. Even though over-the-counter inhalers contain small amounts of epinephrine, the use of these devices is not recommended. Frequent use of them will diminish the effectiveness of the drug as well as place stress on the heart.

Possible side effects include restlessness, paleness, headache, nausea, vomiting, urine retention, and a sense of fear. Doctors urge preventive techniques for managing asthma so that the use of epinephrine can be avoided.

Most brand names for this medication include some form of the word *epinephrine.*

Cromolyn Sodium
Originally isolated from an Egyptian weed and used in an ancient remedy, this drug is now available as a synthetic chemical. It has been in use in the United States since the mid-1970s.

Cromolyn sodium is unique among asthma medications for several reasons. For one thing, it is not a bronchodilator. For another, it is mainly a preventive drug. When prescribed for the first time, it may take several weeks before it begins to work. After that, the patient takes cromolyn sodium before the attack occurs. For example, if a patient's asthma attacks occur during exercise, the patient takes the medication fifteen to thirty minutes before the activity. Moreover, cromolyn sodium is one of the safest asthma medications on the market. It has few side effects and does not interfere with other drugs.

Cromolyn sodium is available as an inhalable white powder. Since it does not travel throughout the body, only small amounts of the drug are needed. The disadvantage of cromolyn sodium is that the powder can cause coughing, which then induces wheezing.

Brand names for cromolyn sodium include: Intal, Nasalcrom Nasal Solution, and Opticrom.

Other Bronchodilators

Four additional bronchodilators are now being used—isoetharine, metaproterenol, terbutaline, and albuterol. These drugs are usually inhaled.

Inhaled medications have few side effects, are convenient, and act rapidly. Their main disadvantage is that they require some coordination. Unless the inhalators are properly held, as much as 90 percent of the medicine is absorbed at the back of the throat and never reaches the lungs.

Steroids

A class of drugs known as steroids can have serious side effects, such as cataracts, osteoporosis, weight gain, high blood pressure, and muscle weakness. For these reasons, they are prescribed only when a patient's asthma symptoms are completely unresponsive to other medications. In many of these cases, steroids are extremely effective. Taken orally in small doses and for short periods of time, the side effects are min-

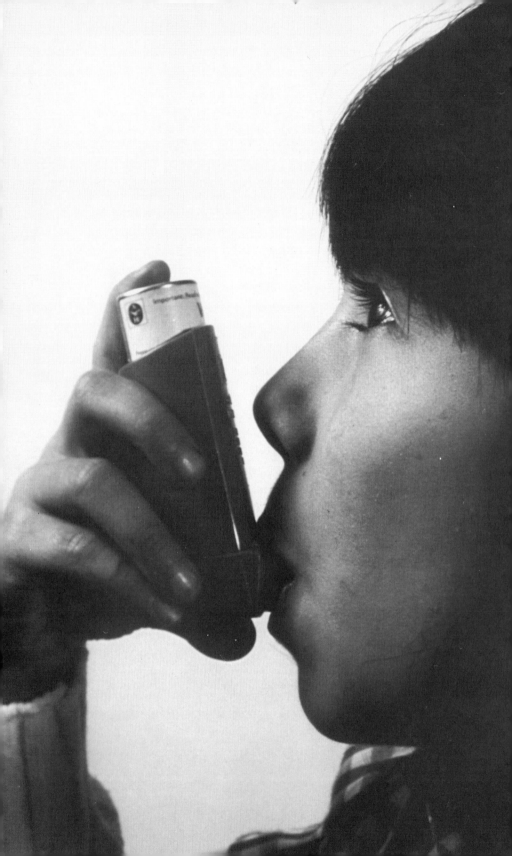

imized. Inhaled steroid medications are much safer; none of the above side effects are known to occur when the medication is inhaled.

Allergy Shots
If it is definitely established that asthma symptoms are a result of an allergic reaction and the allergen cannot be avoided, then allergy shots occasionally may be used as a treatment. Because allergy shots consist of potent extracts of the allergen only, they are rarely used as the sole medication for asthma.

Coping with Mucus
One disagreeable symptom of an asthma attack is thick, bronchial mucus. To some extent, theophylline and inhaled drugs relieve the patient's discomfort. In addition to these, there are other drugs that specifically help clear mucus. *Antibiotics* fight infections and make the thick mucus easier to cough up. *Dilutents,* such as water or a salt solution, increase the water content of mucus. *Surfactants* weaken the stickiness of mucus in much the same way that soap weakens the grease on dirty pans. *Bronchomucotropics* are aromatic inhalants such as eucalyptus, menthol, or *Vicks Vapor*

With bronchodilators, the user inhales a drug that dilates bronchial muscles, allowing air to pass to the lungs.

Rub. There is no proof of the effectiveness of this last group, but many people report that their symptoms are relieved by them.

Over-the-counter Medications

For light, occasional bouts of asthma, over-the-counter medications are fine. However, they must not be used frequently or they will lose their effectiveness. Also, serious side effects are associated with the heavy use of these drugs. In the treatment of asthma, it is best to rely on a physician's recommendations.

Alternate Treatments

When people don't feel well, they will try nearly anything. Occasionally, the unusual treatments actually relieve some symptoms. In many cases, however, the treatments waste time and money.

You might have heard of a "friend of a friend" who tried one of the following treatments and it worked. It's possible. Still, most physicians do not recommend such methods.

Acupuncture

Acupuncture is an ancient Chinese treatment involving needles inserted into specific parts of the body to relieve pain and to cure diseases such as arthritis, asthma, migraine headaches, and ulcers.

According to the Chinese, energies flow through the body in twelve paired and two unpaired "meridians." Different points on the skin correspond to specific energies. One or even hundreds of needles may

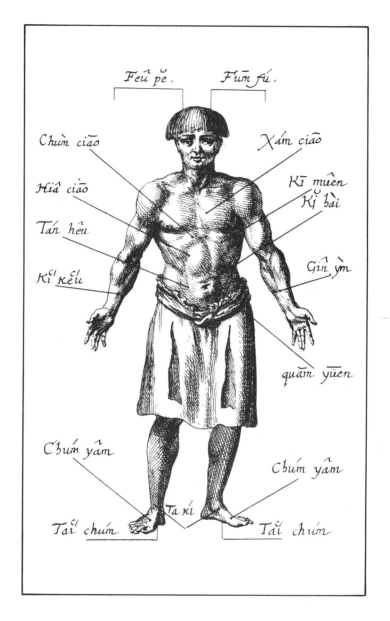

An ancient Chinese chart shows the points
on the skin to be treated in acupuncture.

be inserted into the skin. During surgery, Chinese physicians often use acupuncture instead of giving the patient an anesthetic. Medical evidence suggests that acupuncture increases the brain's production of natural painkillers called *endorphins*.

Several sensations are usually experienced in an acupuncture treatment. At first, a sharp pinch is felt. This is followed occasionally by a tingling. As long as the needles are in place, there is a sensation of numbness, heaviness, or soreness.

Although acupuncture has been practiced widely in the Far East for thousands of years, it's only been practiced in the United States since the 1970s, though with some positive results. Some American physicians report that asthma patients experience a small improvement in breathing and a decreased need for medication. Still, acupuncture is not fully accepted as a form of medical treatment in the United States.

Herbalism
Herbalism is the study and use of herbs, especially for medicinal purposes. Throughout the centuries, herbs have been a mainstay in medicines. In fact, one of the best asthma medications currently on the market—cromolyn—comes from an Egyptian weed.

Before treatment, a herbalist records a detailed history of the patient. Then the herbalist usually recommends a program of diet, exercise, and herbal treatment.

Many herbs relieve asthmatic symptoms. To relieve coughing and get rid of mucus, herbalists recommend teas made of mullein, elecampane, ephedra, eucalyptus, horehound, lungwort, and pleurisy root. An infusion of garlic, ground ivy, blackthorn, and blue vervain, or of yerba santa, cayenne, gum plant, vervain, and blackthorn relieves spasms.

Although physicians recognize the usefulness of herbs, they are quick to point out that they are not as powerful or as fast-acting as modern medications. Herbalists agree that this is true, but they claim, without offering proof, that herbs are ultimately more effective because they strengthen the body.

Homeopathy
Homeopathy is a method of treating diseases by giving the patient small doses of a substance that in large doses would make a healthy person sick. In homeopathy, rashes are treated with doses of poison ivy. Colds are treated with onions, since onions cause crying and a watery discharge from the nose. Allergy-shot treatments operate under a similar premise. Small doses of the allergen are injected into the patient, which should, over time, result in a greater tolerance for the allergic substance.

First developed by the German physician Samuel Hahnemann in the late 1700s, homeopathy practice requires that only one treatment be tried at a time. If the symptoms do not disappear, then subsequent treatments are tried until the illness is cured.

It has never been proven scientifically that homeopathy is an effective medical alternative. Critics complain that homeopathic treatments are far too slow and that many of the treatments could be hazardous if the offending substance is taken in large-enough doses.

Naturopathy

Naturopathy is a system of therapy in which natural things such as fresh air and exercise are preferred to drugs. Many of the practitioners refer to themselves as holistic healers. Holistic healers don't treat the symptoms of a disease. Instead, they attempt to treat the whole individual. Most doctors claim that asthma treatment is beyond the capabilities of holistic healers.

Chiropractics

Chiropractics is the treatment of disease by manipulating the spine and other parts of the body in the belief that many diseases result from undue pressure on nerves. Physicians as well as many chiropractors refute the notion that chiropractics can help asthma patients. However, many persons with asthma report that their symptoms improve after a treatment. This may occur because the chiropractic treatment relieves stress or tension.

Hair Analysis

Hair analysis is a test designed to measure an individual's nutritional health. The hair is first washed, and a portion of the scalp is shaved. No chemicals of any kind are used on the hair. This area must not be washed until new hair is grown. The newly grown hair, free of any chemicals, is then analyzed.

When performed correctly, this procedure can provide an accurate nutritional analysis. Unfortunately, many hair-analysis clinics analyze hair straight from the patient's head. Shampoos and hair sprays distort the nutritional analysis.

Although hair analysis has been recommended to many asthmatic sufferers, no scientific research exists to support the idea that asthma is caused by a nutritional deficiency.

Cytotoxic Testing

The premise of cytotoxic testing is that asthma symptoms result from a toxic reaction to particular foods or chemicals. To conduct the test, a blood sample is taken from the patient. The white blood cells are removed from the sample and mixed with extracts of foods and chemicals. If the white cells appear to die, the patient is said to be allergic to that substance.

Cytotoxic testing is a fraud. It does not work. It has been condemned by the American Academy of Allergy and Immunology as well as by the U.S. Food and Drug Administration.

Vitamin Therapy

Some vitamin therapists claim that asthma sufferers have a genetic disorder that affects their metabolism and that leads to a vitamin and mineral deficiency. Even though this theory has not been proven scientifically, physicians suspect that people with asthma may require more vitamins than normal people. Therefore, physicians often recommend that asthma patients take a daily multivitamin.

CHAPTER

4

EXERCISE

For many people with asthma, the mere thought of exercise is terrifying. Unfortunately, in the past, doctors often recommended that asthma patients avoid exercising. Today, we know this is not good advice.

Before you begin any exercise program, discuss it with your doctor. By working together, both of you can design a plan that fits your individual needs.

Research shows that during vigorous exercise, a person with asthma can have an attack. Naturally, anyone would want to avoid a painful or scary experience. However, many problems develop when children avoid sports or exercise. For one thing, they lose a sense of control over their own lives. Secondly, they lose self-esteem every time they say, "I can't." Most importantly, their bodies don't become strong. And children who are physically fit cope better with asthma than do children who are not.

Many athletes have successfully learned how to cope with their asthma. As a result of their physical-fitness program, their heart, lungs, and muscles have grown stronger, and they do not have to strain to breathe. Another positive result of training is that exercise-induced asthma attacks become less severe. Interestingly, people with asthma discover that they breathe easier during exercise than when they are at rest. Perhaps this is because the hormone epinephrine, released during exercise, opens up airways.

Continuous and strenuous exercise can provoke asthma attacks. An asthma attack usually peaks five or six minutes after the exercise is finished and lasts from thirty to sixty minutes.

Research studies conducted on asthma patients using treadmills found that attacks are likely to occur within six to eight minutes of starting. If the patient stopped before this time period, an attack was often prevented. If the patient continued even while experiencing the attack, he or she occasionally ''ran'' through it.

Still, a fast 1-mile (1.6-km) walk is more likely to produce wheezing than a 50-yard (46-m) jog followed by rest, then followed by another jog. Therefore, repeated, interrupted exercise sessions are recommended for people with asthma.

Although asthma sufferers should avoid long-distance running and scuba diving, they can play any sport that does not require continuous exercise. Appropriate sports include swimming, baseball, football, golf, tennis, or weight-lifting (for adults only).

(53)

Suggestions for Preventing Exercise-Induced Attacks

- Take prescribed medications fifteen to thirty minutes before a workout.
- Do warm-up exercises fifteen to twenty minutes before the vigorous exercise.
- Don't exercise for more than thirty to forty-five minutes. Alternate periods of rest and activity.
- Breathe through your nose.
- In cold weather, use a facemask or scarf.
- If you suffer from environmental allergies, don't exercise outside when the pollen count is high.
- After a workout, cool down for ten to thirty minutes. Appropriate activities are slow jogging, stretching, or light weight work.

CAUTION: If you are taking oral steroids or other heavy medications, do not exercise without first checking with your physician. Too much stress could be placed on your heart and lungs.

Breathing Exercises

In addition to striving for overall physical fitness, asthma patients need to practice breathing. The fear of not being able to get a breath causes them to tense their bodies and take quick, shallow breaths. Instead of using all of their lung power, they use only their upper lungs. As a result, they strain the muscles in

Young patients at an asthma treatment center compete to see who can blow the paper ball the farthest as an exercise to improve lung capacity.

their neck and upper chest. In most people, the diaphragm does 65 percent of the work by pushing against the lungs to exhale and lowering to inhale. The diaphragm of an asthma patient may do as little as 30 percent of the work. Breathing exercises help asthma patients to (1) control and coordinate their breathing, (2) increase their air supply, and (3) strengthen their abdomens. In addition, breathing exercises are strongly recommended during an acute asthma attack because they help relax the muscles.

Here's an effective breathing exercise:

1. Lie on your back with a pillow under your knees, preferably on a carpeted floor. Place one hand on your upper chest and the other hand on your stomach.

2. Relax your stomach muscles.

3. With your mouth closed, inhale through your nose. If you are breathing correctly, the hand on your stomach will rise. The hand on your chest will not move.

4. Slowly exhale through tightly pursed lips. (Your breath should make a hissing sound as your abdomen lowers.) Do not move your chest.

When this exercise becomes effortless, repeat it in a sitting position, then standing, and finally, while walking. To increase muscular strength, lie on your back and repeat it with a weight on your stomach. Begin with a 4-pound (1.8-kg) weight and work up to 20-pounds (9-kg). (A book makes a good weight.)

Relax stomach muscles.

Place one hand on upper chest,
the other hand on stomach.

air

Inhale through nose only.
Hand on stomach should rise.
Hand on chest should not move.

Exhale slowly through
tightly pursed lips.
Hand on chest should not move.
Hand on stomach should lower.

To increase strength,
repeat exercise with
weight on stomach.

BREATHING EXERCISES

RELAXATION EXERCISES

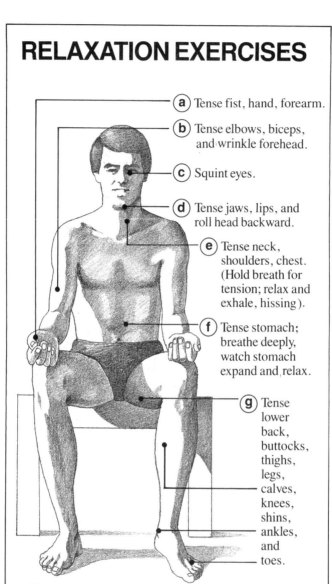

(a) Tense fist, hand, forearm.

(b) Tense elbows, biceps, and wrinkle forehead.

(c) Squint eyes.

(d) Tense jaws, lips, and roll head backward.

(e) Tense neck, shoulders, chest. (Hold breath for tension; relax and exhale, hissing).

(f) Tense stomach; breathe deeply, watch stomach expand and relax.

(g) Tense lower back, buttocks, thighs, legs, calves, knees, shins, ankles, and toes.

Tense each group for five to seven seconds, then relax them for twenty to thirty seconds.

Relaxation Exercises

People with asthma tend to tense their muscles for fear that they won't be able to breathe. Tension tightens the airways and reduces the amount of air that can pass through them. Relaxation exercises help to reduce this stress. Practice the following exercise twice a day for fifteen-minute periods. In addition, the breathing exercise just described can also be used as a form of relaxation exercise:

1. Either lie down or sit in a chair.

2. Tense each group of muscles for five to seven seconds, then relax them for twenty to thirty seconds. Concentrate on how you tense up and relax, so that you can learn how to control relaxation. Go in this order:

   a. fist, wrist, and forearm (first one side, then the other)
   b. elbows, biceps, and forehead (wrinkle forehead)
   c. eyes (squint)
   d. jaws, lips, and head (roll head backward)
   e. neck, shoulders, and chest (Hold breath for tension, then relax and exhale, making a hissing sound.)
   f. stomach (Then breathe deeply and watch stomach expand and relax.)
   g. lower back, buttocks, thighs, legs, calves, knees, shins, ankles, and toes.

CHAPTER

5

PREVENTING OR
CONTROLLING ATTACKS

Asthma isn't curable, but it can be effectively treated and attacks prevented in many cases. Oddly enough, some people choose not to take steps to prevent their attacks. "I was embarrassed to use my medications in front of my friends," they say. "Only sissies practice relaxation exercises"; "I don't need my medicine anymore because I'm better"; or "It was just a tiny little kitten." Unfortunately, such excuses often result in severe attacks.

Avoiding Asthma Triggers

Many asthma attacks are caused by asthma sufferers not taking their medication as directed. They either don't take it at all, take too little, or take too much. Remember: Follow your doctor's instructions and take your medicine.

Another medical safeguard includes methods to decrease the likelihood of catching an infectious disease. As mentioned in a previous chapter, viral infections can cause asthma symptoms. One method of protection is the annual flu shot. Although it's true that occasionally people experience flu-like symptoms after taking the shot, its effectiveness is proven. However, asthma patients should avoid the flu shot if they are allergic to eggs. (The vaccine is grown on egg proteins.)

Another method of protection is amantidine. Doctors prescribe this antiviral drug when an asthma patient has been exposed to influenza A or has flu symptoms. To prevent pneumonia in high-risk patients, doctors prescribe a pneumococcal vaccination.

In addition, people with asthma should avoid taking aspirin and products that contain aspirin. Above all, asthma sufferers should never take sedatives. There's a possibility that these may cause breathing to stop permanently.

The most effective method to prevent an asthma attack caused by allergens is simple yet not always possible to accomplish: Avoid the allergens completely. In the past, some people tried to solve this problem by moving to a different part of the country. But this isn't always practical and doesn't even always work. Sometimes the asthma sufferer may merely be exchanging one set of asthma triggers for another.

A third option is to take immunotherapy, or allergy shots. Your attacks, even if you still have them, will be less severe. Not all experts recommend these,

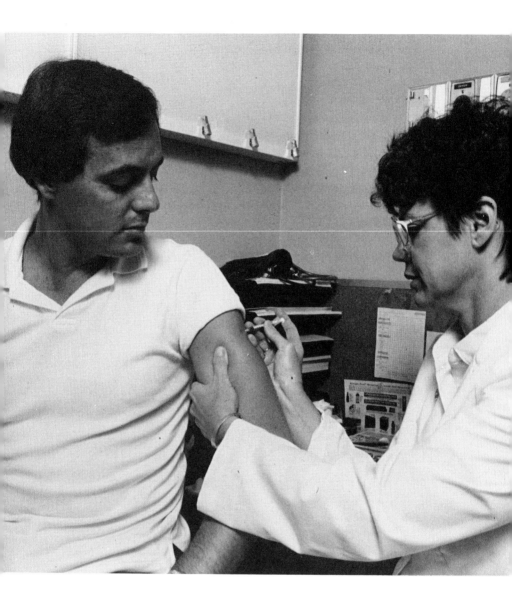

*Allergy shots are sometimes included
in an asthma treatment program.*

however, because only about 25 percent of people with asthma suffer from allergy-triggered asthma; treatments take three to four years; and satisfactory results are not guaranteed, especially for food allergies. But for some asthma sufferers, immunotherapy can be one part of an overall approach to control the disease.

For those with environmental allergies, it is also helpful to:

- Identify your allergens through skin testing, a bronchial provocation test, or providing a complete medical history. Although you may not be able to eliminate your exposure to them completely, you can reduce your exposure to them.
- When conditions outside are poor—for example, when there is a high pollen count—stay indoors as much as possible.
- If you must be outdoors, wear a mask.
- Sleep with the windows closed and use an air conditioner.

Cleanliness is the most effective safeguard against indoor allergens such as household dust, mites, animal dander, molds, and odors. Begin in the bedroom, since this is where you spend the most time. The way in which you clean is more important than how vigorously you clean. For example, keep vacuuming to a minimum because it stirs up dust. Clean with a damp cloth. Wipe baseboards behind the bed and clean the floor underneath the bed. Damp mop walls. Because fabric-covered mattresses collect dust, use vinyl mattress covers that completely encase the mattress. Sleep on synthetic pillows, and wash them monthly. Replace foam pillows yearly. Launder blankets monthly. Do not sleep with quilts; they collect dust. Avoid stuffed toys.

Because mold can grow in plants and in soil, don't keep houseplants. Have leather- or vinyl-covered furniture; if this is not possible, steam clean upholstered furniture and cover it with plastic slipcovers. Avoid rugs or use synthetic or cotton rugs. Avoid heavy drapes over windows. Choose Venetian blinds instead. Change air filters frequently. While cooking, use an exhaust fan. Don't use aerosol spray cans. Eliminate strong odors, smoking, and fires in the fireplace. Do not stay in the house while vacuuming is going on. Keep the temperature between 65° and 70°F (18°C and 21°C). Clean mold-prone areas—refrigerators, garbage containers, and shower curtains—regularly with a fungicide such as Lysol or Clorox. Since mold penetrates plaster, consider painting walls with mold-resistant paint. The last safeguard may be one of the hardest to obey: Don't keep furry pets.

Techniques to Control Asthma

In addition to avoiding environmental triggers, there are specific techniques that can help control asthma. Be as physically fit as possible. Eat a healthy diet and avoid foods that provoke asthma symptoms.

Outdoor activities, often sponsored by asthma treatment centers, promote fitness and friendship.

Read widely and learn everything you can about the disease. If you still have questions, call 1-800-222-LUNG. This toll-free number is sponsored by the National Jewish Center for Immunology and Respiratory Medicine, which is located in Denver, Colorado. The national hospital there—the only one of its kind in the world—treats asthma, respiratory allergies, and immune-system disorders. When you call, expect competent and caring help. Registered nurses trained in specialty areas answer some one thousand calls weekly. The phone lines are staffed 8:00 A.M. to 5:00 P.M., Mountain Time, Monday through Friday. If you dial after hours, leave a message and a nurse will return your call.

Finally, a compassionate support group can be invaluable. Find a doctor you respect and trust. Remember that asthma is not a self-help disease. Be informed and be willing to assume responsibility, but discuss everything with your doctor and follow medical instructions faithfully.

Other members of the support group include your parents and family. Asthma is a chronic disease that affects not only you but also the people around you. Occasionally family members are not as patient or as kind as they should be. Make certain they have adequate information. Always communicate your needs clearly and courteously.

You may find that some of the most helpful members in your support group are other people who have asthma. With them, you can exchange information and openly share your feelings.

Predicting an Asthma Attack

The first step in controlling asthma is to avoid asthma triggers. The second step is to learn how to predict the asthma attack. To do this, you must learn how to listen to your body. There will be early warning signals, and if you pay attention to them, you should be able to avoid the severe reactions associated with an attack.

The Asthma Warning Signals Checklist at the end of this chapter identifies some of the major bodily changes that precede an attack. Photocopy the chart and complete Column #1 for your last attack. (Do not write in this book.) Then, keep a record of the next three times you have an attack. Note any recurring patterns and use these to forecast your future asthma attacks.

When Asthma Flares

During an asthma attack, symptoms rapidly grow worse. Suddenly, the medication doesn't help. There's increased coughing, wheezing, and sticky mucus. Breathing changes. Many attacks occur at night or in the early morning hours, from 7 A.M. to 12 P.M. (People with asthma generally feel better later in the day. Sleeping may alter the body's breathing rhythm.)

At such times, you may not be thinking clearly. For this reason, a written plan is essential. With your doctor's help, make a detailed list of actions you should take. Give a copy of this list to your family, your teachers, and close friends. Keep a supply of backup medications and a summary of all your medications—names, amount of doses, how frequently you take them, and potential side effects. State when to call the doctor and when to seek emergency help. General procedures include:

1. Try to relax. If the attack occurs at night, theophylline and a bronchodilating inhaler may be sufficient to control it. Begin your breathing and relaxation exercises.

2. Do not increase prescribed amounts of drugs.

3. Try to cough up mucus. Drink plenty of water; it helps bring up the mucus. If you are vomiting, the water will keep you from becoming dehydrated.

4. Take your temperature.

5. Monitor your respiration rate. Normal adults breathe at a rate of sixteen to twenty breaths per minute. Infants take thirty-five to forty breaths per minute. If respiration rate remains elevated, seek medical help.

6. Measure your breathing strength with a Peak Flow Meter. This device measures the flow of air from the lung and is often used to monitor the effectiveness of

A Peak Flow Meter
is used to measure
breathing strength.

medical treatment and gives early warnings of asthma episodes. Breathe as hard and as fast as you can into the 6-inch (15-cm) instrument. If your breathing drops more than 20 percent of your normal capacity, seek help.

Postural Draining Technique

People with asthma are sometimes bothered by excess mucus in their lungs. Postural drainage helps to loosen this stubborn mucus in a technique that combines the forces of gravity, clapping, and vibrating. The postural drainage technique is used only when there is a large amount of mucus present. A trained person performs the procedure while the patient rests in one of eight different positions. These positions assume different angles that correspond to the angles of the bronchial tubes. It is not necessary to do all eight positions. It may take some time, after the procedure is completed, before all of the mucus is coughed up.

Here's what happens during the procedure:

1. Before beginning the technique, the patient drinks a large amount of water, in order to lubricate the mucus.

2. The patient stays in one position for two or three minutes.

3. With a cupped hand, the helper rapidly claps the specific area for one minute. The arm moves from the elbow as the hand produces a hollow sound.

4. The helper vibrates the area by rapidly shaking the hand on the area in the direction of gravity. This continues for one or two minutes, until the patient has exhaled five times.

Do not attempt this technique without first being shown how to do it by a doctor or trained person.

Dos and Don'ts

This chapter has described ways either to avoid an asthma attack or reduce its severity. As a quick review, look over the following list of dos and don'ts:

Do secure your doctor's approval for any plan of action.
Do keep a plastic cover on your mattress.
Do change bed linen often.
Do keep air conditioner filters clean.
Do vent cooking odors.
Do keep refrigerator trays clean.
Do keep windows closed during the height of the allergy season.
Do know the names and dosage amounts of your medications.
Do keep a supply of your medications.
Do follow your doctor's instructions carefully.
Do take your medication.
Do know the ingredients of the foods you eat.
Do stay away from people who have colds or the flu.
Do drink plenty of liquids.
Do learn breathing and relaxation exercises.
Do learn everything you can about asthma.

Asthma Warning Signals Checklist

Check any symptom that occurred twenty-four hours or less before the attack.

Type of Reaction	Signal	Attack # 1	2	3	4
Pulmonary	Tightness in chest				
	Shortness of breath				
	Wheezing				
	Coughing				
	Mucus in chest				
Ear, Nose, & Throat	Runny nose				
	Nasal congestion				
	Earache/inflammation				
	Scratchy or sore throat				
Psychological	Irritable				
	Hyperactive/excitable				
	Anxious/depressed				
Other	Headache				
	Tiredness/fatigue				
	Muscle pain/cramps				
	Restless sleep				

(Based on the Asthma Early Warning Indicator in *Asthma, Stop Suffering and Start Living* by M. Eric Gershwin and E. L. Klingelhofer.)

Do know the location and telephone number of the nearest hospital emergency room.

Don't smoke or stay around smoke.

Don't keep furry pets.

Don't spend much time where animals are kept.

Don't remain in your house while it is being painted.

Don't do heavy housecleaning, vacuuming, or dusting yourself.

Don't wear cologne.

Don't use perfumed tissues.

Don't be embarrassed to take your medication in public.

Don't take aspirin or aspirin compounds if you're allergic to them.

Don't eat too fast.

Don't use drugs such as cocaine.

CHAPTER

6

SPECIAL PROBLEMS

Asthma sufferers have one cardinal rule—keep the asthma under control. And, as discussed in the preceding chapter, this is best accomplished by following a careful plan.

Situations occasionally arise, however, that pose additional risk to the person with asthma. These include pregnancy, surgery, and acute asthma attacks. But an awareness of the risks—having accurate information and knowing what to expect—can minimize possible dangers.

Pregnancy

Recent research indicates that with proper medical care, pregnant women who have asthma are not likely to experience more complications than other women. In fact, during pregnancy, one-third of expectant mothers report an improvement in asthmatic symptoms. However, one-third of expectant mothers report that their asthma worsens, and the remaining one-third report that their asthma remains the same.

Still, there are possible risks to the fetus. Asthma slightly increases the risk of premature birth, still-birth, and a lack of oxygen to the developing fetus. Too little oxygen seriously endangers the fetus. This is why women with asthma must try especially hard to prevent asthma attacks during the time of their pregnancy.

Another risk for the fetus is medication. Because doctors fear the possibility of abnormalities in the un-born child, the use of most drugs during pregnancy is discouraged, and therefore we don't know for certain which asthma drugs are safe.

However, some drugs seem to be safer than oth-ers. To prevent asthma attacks, doctors often pre-scribe theophylline, which is believed to increase oxygen to the fetus. If the asthmatic symptoms are not under control after the fourth month of pregnancy, small doses of cromolyn sodium or an inhaled steroid may be prescribed. Small doses of these medications are relatively safe and certainly less dangerous to the fetus than an asthma attack.

After the baby comes, mothers who are breast-feeding and who are taking theophylline may want to decrease their dosage if they notice that the baby is irritable or restless.

To avoid risks in pregnancy, women should take several precautions:

1. Get in good physical shape.

2. Work as a team with your gynecologist or obstetrician and your asthma doctor. Both physicians must be told of the medications you are taking.

3. Avoid infections.

4. Take small doses of asthma medications. Avoid antibiotics, cough medicines, and nasal sprays with antihistamine.

5. Avoid vigorous exercise, climbing to high altitudes, or flying in an aircraft without an extra supply of oxygen.

Surgery

A person with asthma can safely undergo surgery as long as a few simple procedures are followed. First of all, tell your doctor, dentist, and any nurses that you suffer from asthma. Any time surgery is scheduled, get your lungs in good shape by practicing breathing exercises. Also, try to avoid stressful situations. Find out whether or not you can continue your regular asthma medication; make certain the staff knows of any medication you're taking.

Certain anesthetics are best avoided. Cyclopropane, a pulmonary (lung) anesthetic, is not used, since it can produce irregular heartbeats in people taking asthma medication. The barbiturate theopental is also avoided, since it can cause coughing or bronchial spasms. Nitrous oxide, more commonly known as laughing gas, makes asthma worse. Finally, Novocain

A Medic-Alert bracelet ensures that the person's medical history will be available if needed.

is avoided. This local anesthetic is sometimes used for minor surgery and dental work and can cause allergic reactions ranging from hives to the deadly anaphylaxis.

During times of stress, such as surgery, the body releases steroids. If you've taken steroid medication in the past year, your body might not release its own steroids. Then you might need a medical dose of steroids before and after surgery.

Serious consequences can result from an accident if you require emergency surgery and are unable to tell the doctor of your asthma. Keep a card in your wallet with the names and doses of any medications you are taking. The best precaution, however, is to wear a Medic-Alert bracelet. This bracelet also tells hospital personnel that your medical history is kept on a central computer so they can call and receive the necessary information. (Applications for the bracelet are available from your doctor's office or by writing Medic-Alert Foundation, P.O. Box 1009, Turlock, California 95381.)

Acute Asthma Attacks

Acute asthma attacks require emergency treatment. When you have one or more of the following symptoms during an attack, seek immediate medical attention: (1) fever; (2) vomiting and abdominal pain; (3) a persistent, fast respiratory rate; or (4) wheezing that does not respond to normal medication.

Before you leave, call the emergency room (ER) of the hospital so that the staff will be expecting you. Use an emergency room where your doctor is affiliated. Notify your doctor according to your pre-established plan.

Once you arrive at the ER, your treatment will follow relatively standard procedures. Above all, remain calm. Don't be surprised if the ER staff appears unfriendly. They may be very busy, and ER staff are not noted for a gentle bedside manner. What's more, be prepared to wait.

A nurse will examine you by taking your heart rate, blood pressure, respiratory rate, and temperature. Because the nurse decides who is most in need of immediate medical treatment, describe exactly how you're feeling. Also, the nurse will want to take your medical history. Be prepared to give an accurate account of the medications you're taking. You might show the information you keep in your wallet or on your Medic-Alert bracelet.

Next, the doctor will examine you to determine the best medication. At this time, the doctor may order an X ray and an arterial blood gas test. The X ray will show if pneumonia or a collapsed airway is present. The blood test measures the severity of the asthma attack by assessing the amount of oxygen that is in the blood.

Most likely, however, you will be given epinephrine. Younger children receive shots; older children and adults inhale the medication. Within a matter of seconds, there should be a dramatic improvement in symptoms. Almost always, this one dose stabilizes the acute asthma attack.

When this fails, further steps are taken. Oxygen may be required. The doctor usually prescribes inhalation therapy followed by epinephrine. No more than three doses are given, since it increases heart rate and causes nausea.

If this is not successful, the patient is hospitalized and diagnosed as having *status asthmaticus*. This term is used to describe severe asthma symptoms that may be life-threatening. The symptoms include intense constriction and inflammation of the airways; extreme difficulties in breathing; and painful mucus plugs in the airways.

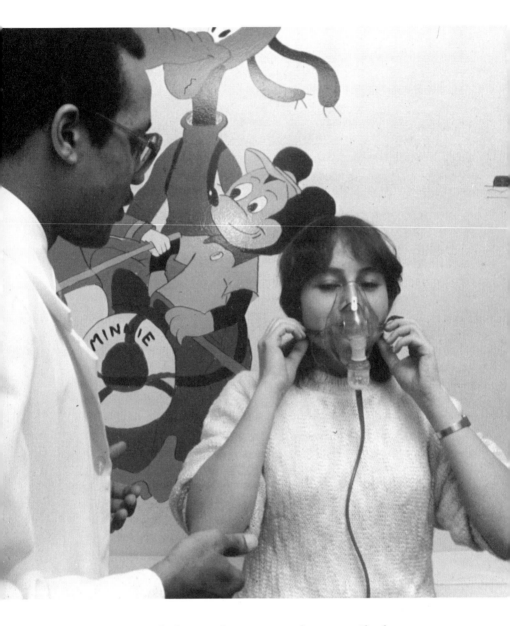

*Inhalation therapy may be prescribed
after an asthma attack.*

At this stage, drastic measures are taken. Drugs such as theophylline are administered intravenously. Also administered are fluids that keep the body from dehydrating. Additional medications are prescribed for coughing. The bronchial tubes may be suctioned with a small instrument.

Doses of steroids are injected. If the doses are too small or stopped too soon, a relapse will occur, worse than the first attack. Because a patient with status asthmaticus is vulnerable to new attacks, a three- or four-day stay in the hospital is common.

Fortunately, few asthma patients are diagnosed as having status asthmaticus. In fact, of all the asthma sufferers in the United States, only 3 percent must be hospitalized. The typical adult who is hospitalized is likely to be a woman between the ages of twenty and twenty-nine. The typical child is likely to be a boy under the age of six.

Although rare, status asthmaticus can be fatal. Generally, a person who dies from an asthma attack (1) has had asthma for more than twenty years; (2) has poorly controlled symptoms and requires frequent ER visits; (3) has been previously hospitalized for status asthmaticus; (4) needs large doses of steroids; (5) has great difficulty breathing in the morning, and (6) takes sedatives or tranquilizers.

GLOSSARY

Adrenaline. See *Epinephrine.*

Allergen. A substance that causes an allergic reaction.

Alveoli. The small air sacs in the lungs where an exchange of gases takes place.

Bronchi. Also called the *bronchial tubes.* The large airways of the lungs, measuring from ½ to 2mm in diameter.

Bronchioles. The smaller airways of the lungs.

Bronchodilator. Any substance that widens the lungs' airways by reducing swelling and clogging.

Cilia. Small hairs on the inside of the nose and the lining of the lung that trap foreign particles.

Diaphragm. Dome-shaped muscle used in breathing; it separates the chest from the abdominal cavity.

Epinephrine. Also called *adrenaline.* A hormone released during stress. The drug epinephrine is used during emergency room treatment to stop a severe asthma attack.

Inhaler. A handheld instrument that releases medication into the mouth.

Trigger. The cause of an asthma attack, such as animal dander and exercise.

WHERE TO GO FOR HELP

There are many sources of information on asthma.

The following selection includes sources at the national and local level and addresses for summer camps.

NATIONAL ASSOCIATIONS

American Academy of Allergy
611 East Wells Street
Milwaukee, WI 53202

American Lung Association
1740 Broadway
New York, NY 10019

Asthma and Allergy Foundation of America
N.W. Suite 305
1717 Massachusetts Avenue
Washington, DC 20036

Asthma Project
National Heart, Lung and Blood Institute
National Institute of Health
Building 31, Room 4A21
9000 Rockville Pike
Bethesda, MD 20205

Asthmatic Children's Foundation
Box 568 Spring Valley Road
Ossining, NY 10562

National Foundation for Asthma
Tuscon Medical Center
P.O. Box 42195
Tuscon, AZ 85733

National Jewish Center for Immunology
    and Respiratory Medicine
1400 Jackson Street
Denver, CO 80206

ALLERGY CENTERS AND CLINICS

These centers offer advanced outpatient care for asthma sufferers. Other clinics may be located through local chapters of the
American Lung Association.

Arkansas
University of Arkansas Medical Center
4301 W. Markham Street
Little Rock, AR 72201

California
University of California Hospitals and Clinics
513 Parnassus Avenue
San Francisco, CA 94143

Colorado
National Asthma Center
1999 Julian Street
Denver, CO 80204

(84)

Connecticut
Yale–New Haven Medical Center
333 Cedar Street
New Haven, CT 06510

District of Columbia
Children's Hospital National Medical Center
111 Michigan Avenue
Washington, DC 20010

Florida
William A. Shands Teaching Hospital and Clinics
University of Florida
Gainesville, FL 32610

Illinois
Institute of Allergy and Clinical Immunology
Grant Hospital of Chicago
550 W. Webster Avenue
Chicago, IL 60614

Iowa
University of Iowa Hospitals and Clinics
650 Newton Road
Iowa City, IA 52242

Kansas
University of Kansas College of Health Sciences
and Bell Memorial Hospital
39th Street and Rainbow Boulevard
Kansas City, KS 66103

Louisiana
Tulane University School of Medicine Allergy Clinic
1430 Tulane Avenue
New Orleans, LA 70112

Maryland
Johns Hopkins Hospital
601 N. Broadway
Baltimore, MD 21205

(85)

Massachusetts
Massachusetts General Hospital Clinical
    Immunology and Allergy Unit
Fruit Street
Boston, MA 02114

Michigan
University Hospital
1405 E. Ann Street
Ann Arbor, MI 48109

Minnesota
Mayo Clinic and Foundation
200 First Street, S.W.
Rochester, MN 55901

Missouri
Children's Mercy Hospital
24th Street and Gillham Road
Kansas City, MO 64108

Nebraska
St. Joseph Hospital
601 N. 30th Street
Omaha, NB 68131

New York
R. A. Cooke Institute of Allergy
428 W. 59th Street
New York, NY 10028

North Carolina
Duke University Medical Center
Durham, NC 27710

Ohio
Children's Hospital Medical Center
Elland and Bethesda Avenues
Cincinnati, OH 45229

Pennsylvania
Children's Hospital of Philadelphia
34th Street and Civic Center Boulevard
Philadelphia, PA 19104

(86)

Rhode Island
Rhode Island Hospital
593 Eddy Street
Providence, RI 02902

Texas
University of Texas Medical Branch Hospital
8th and Mechanic Streets
Galveston, TX 77550

Virginia
University of Virginia Hospitals
Hospital Drive
Charlottesville, VA 22908

Washington
University Hospital
1959 N.E. Pacific Street
Seattle, WA 98195

Wisconsin
University of Wisconsin Hospital and Clinic
600 Highland Avenue
Madison, WI 53702

SUMMER CAMPS

Arizona
Friendly Pines Camp
Senator Road
Prescott, AZ 86301

Arkansas
Alders Gate Camp
2000 Alders Gate Road
Little Rock, AR 72205

California
Camp Wheez
American Lung Association of Santa Clara
San Benito Counties
277 West Hedding Street
San Jose, CA 95110

Colorado
Camp Champ
American Lung Association of Colorado
1600 Race Street
Denver, CO 80206

Connecticut
Hemlock's Outdoor Education Center
Jones Street
Amston, CT 06231

Florida
Camp Lake Swan
Florida Lung Association
5526 Arlington Road
Jacksonville, FL 32211

Illinois
Camp Tapawingo
American Lung Association of Illinois
1 Christmas Seal Drive
Springfield, IL 62703

Indiana
Julia Jameson Health Camp for Children
201 S. Bridgeport Rd.
Indianapolis, IN 46231

Iowa
Camp Superkids, YMCA Camp
American Lung Association of Iowa
1321 Walnut Street
Des Moines, IA 50309

Kentucky
Camp Green Shores
Star Route One
Box 261
McDaniels, KY 40152

Michigan
Camp Michi-Mac
23023 Orchard Lake Road
Farmington, MI 48024

(88)

Minnesota
Superkids Camp
YMCA Camp Ihduhapi
Loretto, MN 55337

Montana
Camp HuffnPuff
American Lung Association of Montana
Christmas Seal Building
825 Helena Avenue
Helena, MT 59601

Nebraska
Camp Superkids
American Lung Association of Nebraska
Suite 212
7363 Pacific Street
Omaha, NE 68114

New Hampshire
YMCA Camp Foss
New Hampshire Lung Association
456 Beach Street
Manchester, NH 03105

New Mexico
Camp Superkids
American Lung Association of New Mexico
216 Truman Avenue, N.E.
Albuquerque, NM 87108

New York
Hidden Valley Camp
Sharpe Reservation
Route 3
Fishkill, NY 12524

North Dakota
Camp Superkids
Triangle Y Camp
Lake Sakakawea
North Dakota Lung Association
P.O. Box 5004
Bismarck, ND 58502

Ohio
Camp Allyn
Amelia Olive Branch Road
Batavia, OH 45103

Oklahoma
Camp Supers
American Lung Association of Oklahoma
2442 North Walnut
Oklahoma City, OK 73105

Oregon
Camp Christmas Seal
Oregon Lung Association
1020 S.W. Taylor, Suite 380
Portland, OR 97205

Virginia
Holiday Trails Camp
Route 1, Box 356
Charlottesville, VA 22901

West Virginia
Camp Bronco Junction
R.D. #1
Red House, WV 25168

FOR FURTHER READING

BOOKS

Gershwin, M. Eric, and E. L. Klingelhofer. *Asthma, Stop Suffering and Start Living.* Reading, Mass.: Addison-Wesley, 1986.

Hass, Francois, and Sheila Sperber Haas. *The Essential Asthma Book.* New York: Scribner, 1987.

Plaut, Thomas F. *Children with Asthma* (2nd edition). Amherst, Mass.: Pedipress, Inc., 1988.

Weinstein, Allan M. *Asthma.* New York: McGraw Hill, 1987.

Young, Stuart H. *The Asthma Handbook.* New York: Bantam, 1985.

PAMPHLETS

Alpert, Linda. "Asthma Fact and Fiction," National Foundation/ Tucson Medical Center, P.O. Box 42195, Tuscon, AZ 85733.

"Asthma Alert for Teachers" (ALA #6013), American Lung Association, 1740 Broadway, New York, NY 10019.

"Captain Wonderlung: Breathing Exercises for Asthmatic Children," American Academy of Pediatrics, 611 East Wells Street, Milwaukee, WI 53202.

"Controlling Asthma" (ALA #1125), American Lung Association, 1740 Broadway, New York, NY 10019.

INDEX